Written by Dave Ellison with photographs by Roy Billings
Based on the BBC TV series ALONG THE RIVER and ALONG THE SEASHORE

Printed in Great Britain by Jarrold & Sons Ltd, Norwich
Published for the proprietors by Polystyle Publications Ltd
Temple Chambers, Temple Avenue, London, E.C.4
Trade distributors, The Argus Press Ltd., 12–18 Paul Street, London, E.C.2

SBN 85096 005 3

Spring

One morning soon after sunrise the river took on a strange and wonderful new face. The misty golden sun reached through the branches of the trees and put its mark on the water with its own reflection. A faint mist rose from the surface, hiding for a moment the rich greens and browns of the river-bank but making every plop and swish sound crystal clear. Soon the mist had gone and the river was awake with the green of the trees and the grassy banks leaping into view.

This was Spring. . . .

It was like a new and magic world. The water was so still we seemed to be looking down into the sky. It was all there beneath us in colourful reflection, white clouds against the blue, sky above and sky below. In that moment we had a sense of unreality – a dream feeling. Only the leaves floating on the placid surface showed that we were not really upside-down.

Have you ever been for a row along the river in the spring? It is the best time of all the year to see how nature lives there, how all the animals and birds prepare for the long summer days to come, and how the river is really a very secret little world on its own.

Mark and Bella, my two young friends, spend some very happy times with me in my boat as we go for day-long trips. Would you like to come? Keep very quiet then as we glide through the water and watch each bank. Who would guess that, as we row along, hundreds of little heads hiding in the bushes are turning and watching and wondering . . . "Where are they off to? . . . What do they want along our river?"

Shhush . . . what's that? . . . It's a blackbird, and he's one of spring's earliest workers, flying low across the fields with a worm held tightly in his bright orange beak. With a flutter he disappears in a wayside bush where his nest and newly hatched chicks are hidden. Every year the blackbirds take us by surprise. Their nests are built, eggs laid, chicks hatched and calling for food long before we think that spring has arrived. But spring is here and all the animals and birds are getting ready for it.

The first job that has to be seen to is nest-building. Along the hedgerows, in the thickets, in the trees and down by the river's edge, we can see the signs of home-making. Over there is Mrs Coot. She's one of the many birds that live all their lives in and around the water, and right now she is busy paddling backwards and forwards along the edge of the reeds carrying a small twig, a leaf or maybe an old feather in her beak.

She builds her nest right on the water, held tightly by the reeds which also help to hide it. Soon the little nest will be home to a new family of chicks, and

both the mother and father coot will spend all day long searching for food . . . a tasty reed shoot, a piece of grass, or some of the weeds that grow on the river-bed.

A coot was the first bird we saw when we went out for a row this spring, and I showed Bella how easy it was to distinguish it from other birds. The coot is about the same size as a small chicken, but it has very dark-coloured feathers, almost black, and a small white patch right on top of the head. Coots are very good swimmers and can dive under water and swim for a very long way out of sight. But they don't like being on the land very much, and about the only time you will see them there is when they are sunning themselves along the banks or searching for a juicy shoot of grass for a meal.

But let us continue our journey. As we row along, the smell of the morning river drifts slowly back from the blades

of the damp oars. Nettles and willow-herbs slide past on either side and then, without any warning, a long neck, quickly followed by a slender body, appears out of the water just in front of us. It is a bird, a very beautiful bird that can swim under water like the coot, only this one has been hunting for fish. This is a grebe, a Great Crested Grebe, with a long white neck, a fine head with glistening black ear tufts, a light brown frill round its cheeks and a slender pointed beak.

With just a quick look in our direction the grebe swims away heading towards its nest in the reeds, for this is another bird that builds its home on the water. Before actually starting to build, each grebe has to find a mate, and this is when young Mark and Bella were able to see a very strange and very wonderful dance performed by the grebes. Two birds sat in the water facing each other and started to shake their heads in the air and stretch their long necks, all the time swaying from side to side and making long strange cries, not a bit like a bird's cry at all. Then, having finished

their dance, the two birds started to build their nest, using long pieces of twigs and reeds, clumps of moss, old leaves and anything else they could find to make it nice and snug.

All these pieces are brought together and firmly anchored to the roots of last year's reeds and then the eggs are laid. Both birds take it in turns to sit on them, and while one is away hunting for food, the other is always on guard, watching and waiting. If anyone comes too close, the bird on the nest will cover the eggs with leaves to hide them and quietly slip into the water. By the end of a month the baby grebes hatch out, and in only a few days they can be seen riding around on the backs of their parents like proud little captains sailing their ships across the sea.

Presently we see a little ripple on the water ahead making its way from one bank to the other, and on getting up close we can see that it's a water vole, or what most people call a water rat. This one is very busy, swimming across the river holding a dock leaf between his teeth, his head held well up so that the leaf stays dry. He lands on the muddy bank and runs into the rushes. Soon he reappears and starts to swim back.

He's a sleek brown shape, this vole, misty and long in the water. His small eyes, close together on top of his head, shine with reflected sunlight as he watches our boat. He reaches the other side, runs into a small tunnel in the over-hanging bank, turns round and peeks out. All is clear, so out he comes again. This time he sits up on his hind legs, pulls a long blade of grass towards him and starts to nibble. It is time for lunch.

Watching him from the top of the bank is another furry little animal that likes to munch away at a clump of grass. It is a rabbit having a short break from guarding her young, hidden below the

ground in the warren. Each spring the rabbit builds her nest at the end of a long tunnel. The nest is made of dried grass and wool. The mother plucks the wool from her body, and this keeps all the babies warm and snug. Sometimes she even makes a door to the warren out of mud, and closes it behind her each time she goes out.

But it doesn't always keep out the rabbit's worst enemy, the stoat. The stoat is a long brown furry animal with short legs and a long tail with a black tip. He spends all his time hunting along the hedgerows and the banks for something to eat. Sometimes, if there is a long cold winter, the stoat may change his colour from light brown to white except that the tip of his tail stays black.

There's another animal that lives

along the bank and looks very much like a stoat, only he is much smaller and has no black tip to his tail. He is called a weasel and he is a very tiny creature but full of fight. He spends his time like the stoat, hunting for food.

By now it is almost midday and the heat of the sun is reflected from the surface of the water. Mark and Bella sit back in the stern of the boat and watch the dragonflies as they twitch and turn above the reeds. The tall grass that grows along the bank is shadowed by swarms of insects, and the water shimmers with the footsteps of the water spider. We see a herd of cows who have come down to the river for a cool drink and to stand in the shade of the trees. Further on we pass a fisherman waiting patiently to see what he can catch.

The river widens, the banks recede and dip down. There is more land, more water. Then, suddenly, the black crest of a heron rises from the tall grass. The kinked white neck appears and the great bird walks slowly and a little stiffly towards the river. He steps into the shallows and stands silently on his long slender legs. He peers down into the water with his beady eyes, aloof and remote and truly wild . . . the tall grey fisherman of nature. He moves along the stream, wading with cautious, stealthy steps. He pauses, stands with head and neck stretched out and then . . . he lunges. He moves so quickly that Bella and Mark almost miss what happens. This is the way the heron goes fishing.

Some way down the stream are some tall trees just a little from the water's edge, and high up in the overhanging branches, huddled together like the houses of a small town, are huge collections of sticks and twigs, large round clusters like the wheels of a cart. These are the nests of the heron, and what nests they are! How their owners must have worked to build such fine homes! In fact their nests are so well made that they last for years and years. And every spring the great birds add a small piece here and there, continually making their houses bigger and stronger.

This town of heron nests is called a heronry, and every spring the cock herons gather together on the mud flats of the river. As the sun sinks low in the

evening, they all fly off to the tops of the trees, back to their nests of last season, each one to the same nest that was his before. And then begins a curious song and dance to attract a female heron.

With long neck and pointed beak held up to the sky, each bird starts to call with a deep booming song. At the same time his legs bend at the knees and his body sinks into the nest. Then he slowly opens his beak and, with a sudden jerk, snaps it shut so that it makes a loud "click". Again he lifts his long neck and turns his body round in the large nest, all the time making a strange rattling sound with his beak.

In a day, or perhaps a week, each heron will have a mate, and the busy task of keeping house begins. Soon the eggs are laid and the young family is hatched. Mother and father are hard at work all day long, flying on their great wings down to the river's edge to stand like tall soldiers, eyes piercing the water.

Our boat moves on and the little hill-side wood comes closer and closer. As we glide into the bank, Mark jumps ashore and ties the rope to a small branch. All three of us climb out on to the grassy carpet of the riverside meadow and unpack our picnic basket. It is time for lunch.

Before long, as we eat our sand-wiches and cakes, the greedy little ducks and the large graceful swans come swimming downstream as fast as they can. First to arrive are the ducks and, perhaps, some little ducklings. The most common duck along the river is the mallard. Father mallard is called a drake and he's a very smart gentleman. He has a bright green head, a white ring round his neck, a rich nut-brown breast and a dark tail with curly feathers. The lady mallard is not nearly so smart; her coat is just plain brown. But she's a very good mother, and she makes sure that each of her brood gets a fair share of the scraps of bread that we throw into the water.

Just as the ducks are beginning to feel a little full they hear a loud hiss. The ducks and Bella and Mark look up and see, swimming gracefully towards them, two swans and their babies. The father leads the way, his wings arched in snowy beauty, while mother and the fluffy grey youngsters follow.

Mark can't tell the difference between

the mother and the father, but it is very easy really. Father swan has a deep orange beak, whereas the lady swan has a very pale beak. Usually swans will keep the same mate all their lives, and every year will build their nest in the same place. A swan's nest is very large indeed. It is made of sticks and reeds, pieces of paper, feathers, mud and anything else that the two birds can find, and they build it low down by the water.

Soon the mother hen lays her eggs, sometimes three and sometimes as many as seven, and the two birds take it in turn to sit and keep them warm. After about five weeks the eggs hatch and the nest is full of large bundles of grey fluff. These are the baby swans, or, as they are called, the cygnets. After two or three days they are strong enough to leave the nest and swim up and down the river with mother never far away.

Just as we were getting back into the boat after our picnic Bella saw a silent movement in the long grass near the river-bank. We kept very still and watched. Presently a fat bundle waddled down to the water, took a few sips, turned round and slowly shuffled back into the undergrowth. It was a hedgehog. Bella and Mark watched carefully to see which way she went, and it was not long before she led them to her nest, a small hollow under the roots of a tree. Inside were three baby hedgehogs.

A hedgehog is covered with a tough coat of prickly spines, and at the first threat of danger it curls up into a tight ball with its little nose tucked into its hind feet. And what a surprise for anyone who tries to open it up! For those prickles are very sharp, and it doesn't take an attacker long to wish that he'd never touched it.

It is not very often that you see hedgehogs during the day, so we were very lucky. Usually they only go out hunting at dusk or early in the morning. They spend all day long curled up in their nest, sound asleep.

Our boat moves smoothly over the water. The oars splash and the spray glitters. The morning clouds have passed away and the afternoon is a silent haze of spring. Suddenly we hear a loud "Honk", quickly followed by another, and then another. And as we round a bend in the stream we come face to face with a goose.

This is a Greylag Goose. It's quite a large bird, something like a duck but much bigger, and the feathers are very soft and are often used to fill pillows and cushions.

Geese like to live in large flocks, and sometimes as many as three hundred birds will live around the same small length of river. Unlike some birds that live by the water and spend a lot of time swimming around on it, geese are very happy walking through the meadows and pastures and feeding on the fresh grass and small insects that they find in the undergrowth.

Of course, like most birds in the spring, they are very busy building nests, laying eggs and bringing up their young. Father goose, who is called a gander, is often seen proudly swimming up and down with his family of fluffy goslings.

Another type of goose we often see has a long black neck with white cheeks and light grey wings. This is called a Canada Goose.

Low down almost at the water's edge another little bird is busy bringing home to her nest the last morsels of food before nightfall. This is the tiny wren. Her nest is very well hidden under clumps of earth and grass that overhang the bank, and it is also very well made. With small pieces of moss, grass and leaves, the male wren builds three or four dome-shaped houses, each with a tiny door in the front. As soon as he has finished building one, the lady wren comes to inspect it. If she doesn't like it he builds another one, and this goes on until he has built her one that she likes.

Having made her choice, she goes inside, lays her eggs, hatches them out and then has the hard work of feeding the chicks. The Jenny Wren, for that's what some people call her, is one of the smallest birds in the country.

By now the afternoon is late, and a strange mist seems to drift above the line of trees along the river-bank. It rises and becomes grey against the yellowing sky, and as we row nearer we can see that it is not a mist at all, but a cloud of gnats. Millions of them are dancing together in a smoky haze of movement. Swallows and swifts swoop down to feed on the thicker swarms.

But now it is evening. From our boat we watch the sunset, and as we row back we pass the long shadows of the waiting heron. We smell the rich smell of the land and the damp night smell of the darkening water.

The magic of spring is with us and we know that soon – very soon now – we shall be enjoying the open-air life of summer.

Summer

Now it's time for a holiday down by the sea. Mark and Bella always look forward to this time of year and have great fun playing in the sand, paddling in the warm sea, going for boat trips round the harbour and scrambling over the rocks and round the rock pools.

But, you know, that's not all there is to the seaside. It's not only rocks, sand, sea and boats, it's very much more than that . . . it's the home of more animals than any other part of the country. But you have to look very carefully to find them.

The easiest animal to find is the one that is always hidden in its little house. This house is called a seashell, and inside lives a soft and very strange creature. He can live both in the sea and on the shore and is called a shell-fish. His shell is very tough to protect his soft body.

Some shellfish are called bivalves because they live inside two shells hinged together like the lid of a small box. The oyster, the mussel and the razorshell are hinged like this, and when the creature inside wants to eat it opens up the two halves of its house and pushes out its head so that it can catch the tiny pieces of food that float around under the sea.

Other shellfish, like the periwinkle, just have one shell, and some of them look very much like a snail in your garden. Mark and Bella are always exploring the rocks, the breakwaters and the beach under the pier at low tide looking for them. They know that

these are the places where such shell-fish live, hidden amongst the seaweed on which they feed.

The small periwinkle is very tiny indeed. In fact it's just about the size of the tip of your little finger. But it's the common periwinkle that is the one you most often find. It has a thick black shell and is usually just called a winkle and you can buy it in the fish shops, or from the stalls on the promenade, to eat.

But the most beautiful of all the periwinkles are the yellow and pink ones, and these are called flat periwinkles, but I don't know why, because they are not flat at all.

Bella likes to collect these pretty coloured shells, and this summer she is going to keep them in a special box so that she can show them to her friends.

If you look closely at the clumps of seaweed along the shore you may find some of the eggs of the flat periwinkle. It lays a cluster of eggs together inside a small blob of jelly which holds them safely on the weed.

All shellfish like to hold tightly on to something, and the one that holds tightest of all is the limpet. Have you ever heard people say "It sticks like a limpet"? Well, when they say that they mean that it is stuck very firmly and no one can move it.

Limpets have a tent-shaped shell and they like to cluster together on the side of a large rock, each holding on with its foot. When they think that no danger is around, or when the sea is covering them, they will lift up their shell, stick out their small head and walk around quite quickly on their one foot hunting for food . . . tiny, short pieces of sea-weed.

When their meal is over a very strange thing happens. Each limpet makes his way home, not just to the rock that it came from, but to the exact spot on the same rock. In fact, because it always goes back to the same place, the limpet wears a little groove in the rock with the edge of its shell, and it is into this that the limpet always snuggles.

If you are very quiet next time you find some limpets on a rock you might see them peeping out at you from under their shells. But make the smallest noise, and . . . Clomp! . . . they bang down their little house harder than ever.

Another animal that lives along the seashore in a shell is the crab. I expect you've seen plenty of crabs when you've been down to the seaside. Mark and Bella certainly have, but Bella isn't too happy about picking them up because she says they might give her a nip. She's right you know, because nearly all crabs have two large legs in front with strong pincers on them, and if you get too close they might well give you a nip. The other eight legs of the crab are used for walking, and he walks in a very funny way – sideways, and quite quickly.

Mark and Bella are always finding empty crab shells on the beach, and they used to think that they were dead crabs. But they were wrong. Most of the empty shells are the ones that the crab has grown out of as he gets bigger, just as you grow out of your clothes as you get older. As a crab gets older he gets too big for his shell, so he takes his old one off and, for a while, his soft body is left unprotected and he has to hide. If he didn't he would soon be eaten up by a hunting fish or a seagull. But very soon his new shell grows and the crab is safe again.

Once when Bella was searching through some thin strands of seaweed in a small rock pool she felt it try to walk away. To her surprise she saw when she looked closely that some of the weed wasn't weed at all, but an animal. It was a spider crab. These crabs have very long legs and a small body and look very much like a piece of seaweed. In fact they often fasten small lengths of real seaweed to their bodies just to help the disguise. They really are very clever, because when they do that you just can't see them at all.

Just after Bella had found the spider crab, Mark noticed some strange blobs of jelly sticking to the wet rocks. Some were quite big, almost as big as his fist,

while others were very small, just about the size of a shirt button. Some were red and some were yellow, and when Mark looked very closely he could see that they were breathing.

I told him to look down into the rock pool to see if he could see any under the water, but although he looked very carefully he couldn't find one. And no wonder. You see, when they are under the water they open up like a flower, and long petal-like arms wave around in the current. These strange little creatures are called sea anemones, and they are not plants at all. The sea anemone is an animal and the petals are its arms. It is with these that it catches its food . . . large anenomes eat small fish, a shrimp or even a tiny crab or periwinkle.

I suppose we always think of a summer day as being hot with a blue sky overhead and the sea rippling gentle waves up to the beach. But it isn't always like that. Sometimes the sky grows dark, the wind starts to blow and the sea changes from blue to grey. It begins to heave up and down in great breaking waves that come crashing up on to the beach with a roar. Then, without pausing for breath, they rush back out to sea again as though to gather strength for their next attack. This is a summer storm.

As the waves pound on the shore, the pebbles and small pieces of rock get rolled backwards and forwards against one another gradually grinding them-

selves smaller and smaller, until, after many, many storms they have been ground up so small they have become sand. And this is how a sandy beach at the seaside is made.

But a summer storm doesn't last long, and very soon we are able to go exploring again.

The waves have left a thick carpet of seaweed all along the shore. There are long brown weeds with crinkly edges which are called sea-belt. There are green weeds with what look like blisters all over them. But these blisters are really small air pockets which help to support the plant as it sways backwards and forwards in the tide. Mark and Bella have great fun bursting these little pockets with their fingers to see who can make the loudest POP. Also along the beach they find long strips of weed that look like shoe-laces only very much longer. This is called thong weed. Then sometimes they find some sea-lettuce, a beautiful plant with thin pale leaves that look more like paper tissue than a piece of seaweed.

Some of the weeds that we find along the seashore are fixed to a small stone with things like roots. But they are not roots at all. They are called hold-fasts, and are really a lot of little fingers that grip firmly to stones and rocks so that the plant stays in one place and doesn't drift off into the current. During a storm some of those that are holding on to just a small stone,

or that lose their grip in the rough water, get washed up on to the beach and die in the sun.

Every now and then, if we look carefully, we might find a starfish. But a starfish isn't really a fish at all. It is a strange animal that lives under the sea and is shaped like a star. Most starfish have five spiny arms, and underneath each arm there are rows of tiny suckers which help it to move about and catch its food. One very odd thing about a starfish is that if it ever loses an arm it doesn't have to worry, because in a very short while it grows a new one.

One day when we were walking along the beach, Bella pointed to something that looked like a ball. But she soon discovered that it wasn't, because it was covered with long spikes that pricked her when she tried to pick it up. It was a sea-urchin, and although it

looks quite different, it belongs to the same group of animals as the starfish.

Have you ever heard of a mermaid's purse? No? Well nor had Bella and Mark until one day, as we searched among the rocks, Mark found a strange little bag with a long curly point on each of its four corners. He was very surprised when I told him that this was an egg.

In fact it is the egg of a baby skate, which is a large flat-fish that you often see in a fish shop. The long curly points on each egg are used for holding on to a piece of seaweed under the water, and in this way the egg is held safely in place until the baby fish hatches out.

The skate's egg that Bella found was black all over. But sometimes you may find a brown one with even longer points. These belong to the dogfish.

Of course, it's not very often that you find fish along the seashore. But if you could go under the water in the rock pools you would be able to see them swimming about all over the place, hunting all the time for something to eat.

The fish you are most likely to see darting about in the pools is the blenny, or, as some people call it, a shanny. This fish is a very good parent, and after the mother has laid her eggs, the father will swim backwards and forwards over them making sure that they are safe. And he will keep on doing this until the little fish hatch.

Other fish will do this as well. The little stickleback even builds a cave-like nest for its eggs and so does the sand goby. Father Goby not only stands guard over his eggs, he also fans them with his fins day after day, swishing clean water in and out of the nest until the day they hatch. Then the little fish swim away and have to look after

Can you find these shells on the beach?

Limpet

Winkle

Razor Shell

Cockle

Slipper Limpet

Mussel

themselves, watching with their big eyes for all the dangers that are hidden beneath the sea. There are dangers for them above as well, dangers that they can't see until it is too late.

The big sea-birds are out hunting for them all day long. One of the biggest birds that we see along the coast is the cormorant. We often see them flying low across the water or standing on the end of the jetty, their heads held high as they peer down into the water, watching for some unsuspecting fish to swim past.

When Mark and Bella come with me for a walk under the cliffs we often see the nests of seagulls, perched high up out of reach on a rocky ledge. Some-

times, if we are lucky, we see the nest of a tern. Terns guard their nests and their young very well, and will chase away other birds no matter how large they are. They only have two or three chicks each year, which is a good thing really, because the young eat an enormous amount, and the parents are kept busy all day long searching for food. Then, as summer comes to an end and the terns fly away with their family, some of them make their way to the other side of the world, 10,000 miles to the Antarctic.

But at home the seagulls stay the whole year through, though some of them move away from the sea and spend the days searching for something to eat in the fields.

Often on a late summer afternoon you will see them flying low behind the farmer's plough, swooping down every now and again to pick up some tasty piece of food that happens to be dug up and lying on the ground.

For by now autumn is on its way and food is not so easy to find. The days are getting shorter and the nights are getting longer. A cool nip is in the air as summer says goodbye, and Mark and Bella go home with many happy memories of our days along the seashore.

Autumn

Summer is gone now, and Mark and Bella are just a little sad. They love the warm sunny days when we can go for picnics. The sun is still bright, and the sky is often blue and clear, but picnics, I am afraid, are out of the question.

Autumn, however, is not really sad. Autumn is simply the season when nature is preparing for her long winter sleep. And the mantle of green that she is casting away now will come back again in spring, a brighter green than ever. Her cloak of golden brown is simply the one she wears in the evening of the year.

On a really bright day, when the air is crisp and cool, Mark and Bella put on their warm winter coats and we go for a walk along the river-bank. We do not take the boat these days because it is warmer walking.

All is silent as we make our way through the dead leaves and bracken that line the river-bank. The crackle of the leaves as our feet swish through them is the only sound that disturbs the stillness.

But the trees are not yet all bare. We can still see some leaves clinging to the branches, a bit yellow and withered, and getting ready to fall. Before it does so, each golden leaf forms a shiny ring of jelly around its stem, and then begins to ease itself away from the branch. Soon a gentle breeze helps it to float away, and one more leaf flutters to the ground.

As we pause to look around, the silence almost makes itself felt, and Mark and Bella stand and listen carefully. Mark wants to know why everything is so quiet.

Well, of course, most of the birds have flown away now, migrating – as we call it – to warmer climates. Nothing stirs except for the few that are still with us, flying from tree to tree as though counting the empty nests left over from the busy days of spring.

But there is still plenty to see if we look carefully. The ducks, the geese and the swans stay with us all the year round, and there are always the fascinating little creatures of the forest.

One little chap who is very busy these days is the cheeky grey squirrel. We might see him climbing from branch to branch high in the tree-tops, or scampering through the fallen leaves and yellowing tufts of grass or fern. All day long he is out and about, searching for nuts, hiding them under leaves, then off again for more nuts. He is storing them up for the winter.

Sometimes it is a hazel nut that he

A SQUIRREL GAME

Here is a dice game for two or more players. Use small buttons as counters. The first player to throw six can start. Score the exact number to finish.

7
8
Chase butterfly Go on to 14
9
10
Short cut Go on to 17
11
12
13
Slip on branch. Go back to 9.
14
15
16
Getting late. Hurry on to 20
17
28
Trip over. Miss a throw
29
30
31
32
Home

finds, sometimes an acorn freshly fallen from the old oak tree. Whatever it is, squirrel knows that he will need all he can get during the long dark months ahead.

But, do you know, he has such a bad memory that he always forgets where he has hidden them. So he still has to spend all winter long hunting for food.

The name 'squirrel' means 'shadow tail', for he has a long bushy tail which he can hold right over his back and even over his head. During the hot summer days he uses it as a sort of sunshade to keep off the sun, and in the winter he can wrap it right round himself to keep warm and snug in the icy blasts of wind.

Sometimes, if we are very lucky, we see a red squirrel, and, if we do, we all keep very still and quiet. We hardly dare to speak. For if we do not frighten him, red squirrel may come right up close to us. But if we make the slightest noise, away he scampers, high up into the trees to hide behind a good thick branch.

Sometimes he will peep out again to see if we are still there.

"Have they gone?" he seems to be asking. "Am I safe?"

He is a nervous little chap and, as soon as he sees us again, he disappears so suddenly we hardly see him go . . . just a flash of nothing.

We like our walks along the river-bank in autumn. Sometimes I think Mark likes them especially because he

so loves to shuffle his feet through the dead leaves. Bella does the same. Then they run and laugh, playing games, and the silence of sleeping nature is broken for a while.

One day they ran ahead and I heard them giggling. They were down among the bushes on the bank, and Mark was pointing to something that amused them both. It was a group of swans, one of whom had thrust its long neck in the water.

Of course, it was searching for food. Throughout the autumn and winter, all wild life must feed. And the waterfowl do not store nuts like the squirrels.

Did you know that swans cannot eat dry food? They always need a little water to drink with it, and you will see them dipping any bread you throw them into the river before trying to eat.

Another thing is, when you see them gobbling the greenstuff that grows along the bank – those weeds that seem to dangle in the water – it is not the greenstuff alone that they are after, but the insect life that it contains.

We always keep a sharp eye open on these walks for the birds that stay with us all the year round, mainly the waterfowl, as I have said, but there are plenty of others.

By now the baby swans of spring have grown almost as big as their parents – not quite as big, perhaps, and certainly not white all over. For they still have a coat of soft grey down, with here and there a few white feathers pushing through, as though to say: "We're here, we're here, just wait till spring." For by then they will be fully grown and white from tip to tail.

Swans are dangerous birds. They are very strong, and you have to be careful of their wings as well as their beaks. They are very easily annoyed too, especially in the nesting season, and they show their feelings very clearly.

An angry swan will shoot out its long, rubber-like neck, hiss, grunt and flap its wings. This is a sign to you to keep clear. I always tell Mark and Bella to keep very clear.

Once I saw a little dog who thought that, swans being birds, he could chase them the way he chased all other birds. He certainly chased away the ducks, for, when he barked and leaped into the water after them, the ducks swam away in great haste.

But the swans were different. They seemed to know that they were royal personages. As the little dog swam towards them, they merely stretched up their long necks, turned their heads round towards him, and seemed to be saying: "Who is this common fellow? What does he want with us?"

Of course, the dog, who was about the size of a terrier, simply wanted to chase them and see them scatter. It was his doggy nature. But the swans did not scatter. They waited till he came up with them, his head just above water as he paddled with his feet, then one of the swans spread out a wing and splashed water all over him.

It must have been a great shock to

the dog. When he had finished gasping, another swan spread its wing and did the same thing. The poor dog had another cold ducking, and seemed a lot less happy when he could be seen again.

After the third splashing, Master Dog turned round and paddled rapidly for the bank. He had had enough of swan chasing. He crawled out, wearing the look of one who had learned his lesson, and trotted off without a single bark.

But it is all right to feed swans by throwing bread to them. They are quite pleased to receive it. And that reminds me that at this time of the year all the birds who stay in this country are very short of food.

All day long they are hunting and pecking at anything that looks good enough to eat. The smallest scrap will please them. From daylight till dark during these short days they spend their whole time searching for something to eat.

The magpie, sitting high up on his branch in the tree-top, looks down with a beady eye. On the ground, not knowing what is in store for it, there may be a snail or an insect. The magpie sees his lunch. With a swoosh he dives from his high branch and snail or insect is gone. That is his lunch. But then it is time for tea. And so it goes on, all day long and every day, because this is the way that nature feeds its creatures.

The magpie is a peculiar bird. It is not always food that attracts him. He is fascinated by anything that shines or glitters in the sun. Often he will make a dive to pick up a bead or a button, a

piece of glass or tin. It is as though he has a fancy for jewels. Then he hides these useless, sparkling things in his secret hoard, but for what reason nobody knows.

As the days grow shorter and the cold winds come down from the north, the wild flowers and plants that grow in such profusion all turn to seed. The seeds fall to the ground, sleep through the winter and come to life again in the spring. This is nature's way of ensuring that life will continue, that nothing will ever really die although it seems to do so, but will be born again in due season.

For example, the willow herb (above), which has a tufted plume that carries its seed high into the sky, gently puts it down along the way to lie in the ground until it is time to root and grow again.

Hidden away almost out of sight by the river's edge among the tall grass is a plant with a very strange name – the roast-beef plant. This is a plant which, during the summer, shows a purple flower and stands tall and proud like an iris in your garden.

But in autumn it puts on quite a different face, a scarlet face of berries clustered on tall stems. This is its garb until the end of winter. And, when that end comes, the berries drop to the ground, to root and grow tall once again in the purple flower of summer.

Even the trees, so big and strong now, grew from tiny seeds. A long time past that old oak, with such gnarled and hummocky roots, was just an acorn, buried by some squirrel who, having forgotten where he had buried it, just left it there without knowing in the least that this again was nature's way of ensuring the growth of the massive oak.

The same thing, of course, applies to the great chestnut tree. Once upon a time it was just a tiny conker. And the tall fir, which stands so straight and tall, was once a small seed hiding in the protective folds of its cone.

Mark and Bella, as they look up, can see these cones high among the branches. At this time of year they are fully grown and almost ready to split open. When they do so, the seeds inside them will fall and make their

simple journey to the ground, where some of them, only a few perhaps, will take root.

Later on the empty cone, having served its purpose, will drop to the ground as well, and there you will find it, lying as though asleep among the fallen leaves.

As the leaves on the trees fade and fall, bright splashes of red and crimson berries warm the bleak and naked banks. We find them almost everywhere.

And when the berries are in full bloom, the little bullfinch is sure to appear. His scarlet breast and smart black head make a brilliant streak of colour as he flies from branch to branch, pecking at a berry here and a berry there.

A few pecks, and away he goes again, across the river and into the woods to search for next year's flowers that lie folded up inside the buds of

trees and shrubs. He is a vegetarian, and these are what he really likes to eat, which is a pity. For every bud he takes means one flower less next spring. But – that's the way that nature feeds its own.

Naturally enough, Mark and Bella like the wild life, the little birds and animals that abound along the river-bank. They like to see them as these lively creatures go about their daily task of feeding themselves. For truth to tell, in this wild life of the woods, finding food is the main necessity. Shelter is needed as well, but nature seems to have fitted its creatures admirably for a life in the open air.

But the children are also interested in the bright berries. The gentle colours of autumn show clearly in the crisp sunlight when the day is bright. And, before our walk is over in these shortening days, I like to show them how the coral-pink berries of the spindle-wood tree mingle in the leafless branches of nature's sleeping garden.

The spindle tree is a tall and slender shrub with a smooth grey bark. In the summer, its branches hold a mass of small white flowers and finely pointed leaves of lightish green.

But now, as always when winter nudges her silent way across the countryside, there comes a change. The flowers have gone, leaving behind them clusters of pale pink fruit. Presently these clusters of berries open up, and each one shows itself to be a cup holding the bright, orange-coloured seed for next year's shrub.

Blending in with the quiet colours of the spindle tree, the rusty, golden fronds of bracken grow like a thick

beside the river, very damp indeed now because the sun has little heat for drying. The winds will come, of course, and play their part in the drying process, but that is not what we are interested in at the moment.

In this damp earth we find many little heads that push their way up towards the light of day. Little heads of toadstools, scarlet and brown, stand like toy umbrellas with nothing to do. Some are very small, and some quite big.

Sometimes when we are looking for

carpet in the filtered light of autumn sun. We stand and gaze awhile, thinking how really colourful this time of the year can be.

But Mark and Bella like to hear of those strange and unexpected things that happen in nature. And when I come across a fallen tree in the woods, I show them how nature clears the ground of things for which she no longer has any use.

This fallen tree is covered now with a mass of yellow heads. And these yellow heads belong to a fungus that is slowly eating away the rotting wood. In the course of time this tree which lies forgotten in the undergrowth, a useless object now in nature's cycle, will be gone. (Picture on left.)

So even a fungoid growth has its purpose. . . .

We walk on along the damp earth

toadstools we find a shaggy ink cap, a most strange plant. It is tall and white with a pale yellow hat. Its body is long and frilly and shaped like a large thimble, and when it is fully grown it starts to curl around the edges. Then it turns black.

Now comes the strange part. Large drops of ink-like juice appear around its rim. Then, the shaggy ink cap falls. Its hollow stem breaks under its own weight. And there, lying on the ground, is just a large black stain.

And that is all that is left of the shaggy ink cap. . . .

Our walk is drawing to an end. We have had a happy day, but it is time to go home. The shades of night are falling, and the evening is likely to be misty. For these days, near the river, there is usually a misty, smoky look about the landscape.

Nature in this season has been preparing to hide her secrets from the winter's cold. And now the night will cover nature. The river ambles on its quiet way to the sea, and we turn and make our way homeward.

It is getting late. There will be other walks on other days, but, for the moment, we leave nature and its teeming but sleeping life to the dark. . . .

Winter

There comes a day now, sooner or later, when we feel a distinct change in the air. Instead of the smell of wood smoke and garden fires we have grown used to at this time of the year, we find suddenly a hard chill striking us.

Gone are the misty but pleasant evenings. Suddenly, we are in the dark nights and short days of Winter.

Let us take one last stroll this year along the river. It is strangely quiet all around, no sound save the crackle and snap of twigs underfoot as we make our way down to the water's edge. And here we are impressed by the stillness.

No insects flutter among the reeds. Few birds call to one another. The bushes that made such brilliant splashes of colour along the banks and in the fields are now stark and naked. It is as though all nature has gone to sleep.

This, in fact, is what has happened.

Let us take another look at those tall reeds. There is a long brown pod at the top, and, if we open it carefully, as Mark did one day, we shall find that it is full of the seeds that are simply waiting there until they can grow next spring. They are surprisingly warm, too, even on a frosty day, for those hundreds of seeds are snugged down in a soft white downy substance.

Nature always finds a way of protecting her young.

The reeds look lifeless, as do the bushes and trees, but they are only biding their time, waiting for the moment when the light and warmth of the sun will waken them to a new life. And plant life is not the only thing that is sleeping.

If we could take a look through some of the dark and mysterious holes and hollows in the trees, we might find some of the little animals that sleep right through the dark days of winter.

One of these is the dormouse. A dormouse is a small rodent, something between a mouse and a squirrel. He has a large head, perky ears and great black eyes. His tail is long, rounded and bushy. His fur is thick, a light yellowish brown on top and whitish underneath.

In the summer the dormouse spends most of the day asleep. In fact he is a very sleepy fellow altogether, because he sleeps more or less right through the winter. It is only at night in the summer that he comes out to hunt for food. Then he collects nuts and seeds and stores them in his nest.

He doesn't eat them all straight away, however, but saves up as many as possible for the autumn. In a way, he is preparing a nice big supper for himself before he goes to bed for the winter. He eats and eats then, gets very fat and finally goes to sleep. Imagine it! He wouldn't say to his friends "See you in the morning", but "See you again when we wake up next spring."

There are other animals that sleep all the winter, and we call them the "hibernating" animals. Hibernation is what we call this long winter sleep.

So far on this winter stroll we have found that the day is frosty but still not the absolute freezing one that comes sometimes during the winter. When that happens we shall perhaps not be able to see the water at all, or only in small patches. It is not often that the weather in this country is cold enough to freeze the river entirely, but we do frequently in very cold weeks find sheets of ice on it.

Now, what happens then to all the birds, the fish and other creatures when their watery home is frozen over?

Well, the fish are quite happy. They still swim lazily about under the ice, finding food as usual among the weeds and so on. They do not often come to the surface anyway. So perhaps the only difference is that they find the light rather darker underwater when there is ice on the top.

But the birds are different. They find the river a strange and awkward place now. No longer can they dive or swim. Sometimes we see them standing about on the ice as though thinking deeply and trying to puzzle out why the water has suddenly become so hard.

The coots, their black bodies standing out sharply against the silvery sheen of the ice, walk with awkward and clumsy steps across it. The ducks, singly or in groups, just stand and stare.

Once when I was with Mark and Bella we saw a funny sight. We watched the ducks coming down in swooping dives and trying to land on the ice as they had been in the habit of landing on the water. The poor ducks were slipping and sliding all over the place. Perhaps it was unkind of us to laugh, but we couldn't help it.

However, as we have said, not all the river is frozen over. Usually there are some clear patches of water in sheltered spots, and here the waterfowl gather in great numbers. The swans, the geese, the ducks and the coots seem only too glad to find these clear patches in which they can dive and swim as usual.

We do not stand for long watching them, because we have to keep warm ourselves. Overhead, the sky is a hard steely colour. We seem to be breathing frost, and our breath comes like steam. So we walk on, glad to keep moving, and glad also that we have a warm home to go back to after this walk in the cold.

Like all other living things we shall be glad when the warm weather comes. At the same time, there is something fascinating about winter. All nature is still, waiting and yet unseen. Unseen like the roots and bulbs of the plants and flowers waiting to push their heads up through the earth and snow, waiting like the crocus and the snowdrop snuggled deeply in the earth, for soon winter will be gone and life will once again stir in every nook and cranny, every field and meadow Along the River

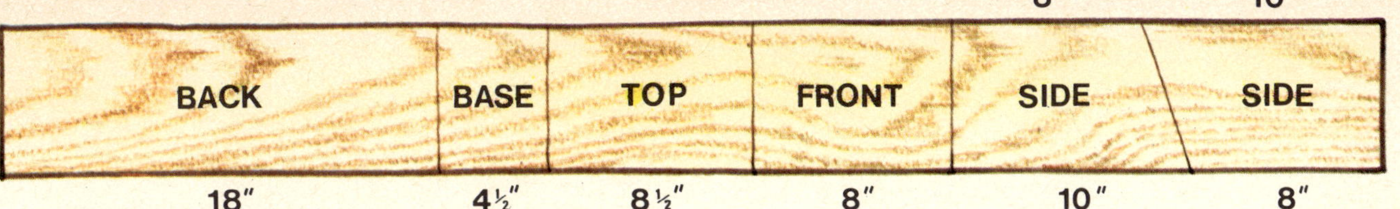

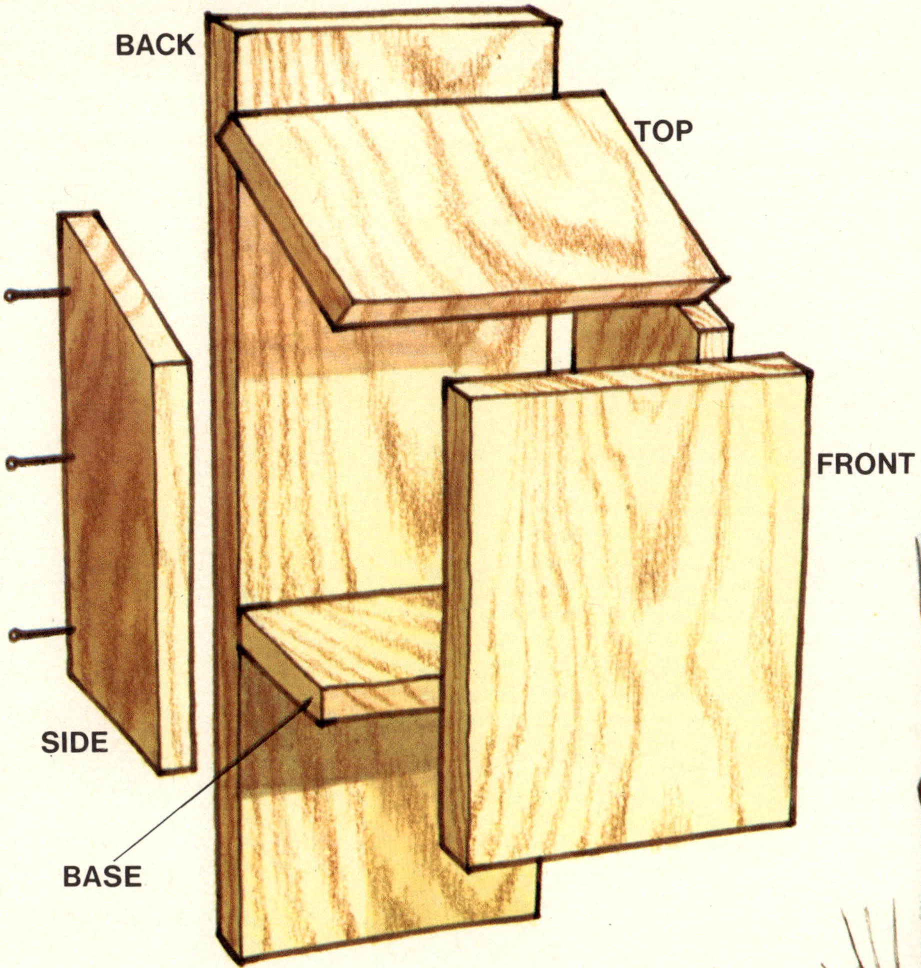

BACK TOP FRONT SIDE BASE

How to make a nest-box to fix in your garden

Materials
One length of deal, 4′ 9″ long, 6″ wide, $\frac{3}{4}$″ thick. A flat strip of rubber, 6″×2″.

Construction
Cut the wood as shown in the diagram. Nail sides to the back. Nail base to the back and sides. Fix rubber strip to the top with small tacks, allowing an overlap to fix to the back. This then acts as a hinge. Drill a hole in the front $1\frac{1}{4}$″–2″ in diameter depending on the type of bird you want to attract. Nail the front to the two sides and base. Tack the other half of the rubber strip to the back. Attach small catches to the two sides to keep the roof firmly in position. Paint the outside with non-toxic preservative.